The Paris Book

by MARIAN PARRY

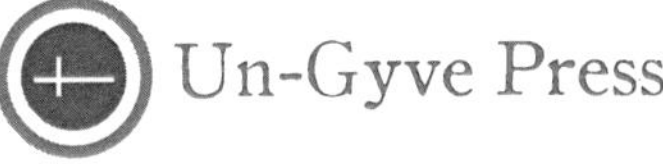

In 1952 Ben Shahn said to Marian Parry, "Marian, make the most beautiful book you can and I'll take it to Curt Valentin." She made *The Paris Book*, which she had conceived of sometime prior to this prompting, and as promised, the book was presented to Curt Valentin who was moved to publish it. Mr. Valentin, who had published several significant, limited edition books in which the writings of poets and novelists were accompanied by illustrations made by contemporary artists, passed away the following year and *The Paris Book* was never published. Un-Gyve now publishes this most beautiful book of watercolours in their exquisite detail exactly as was intended. *The Paris Book* represents Marian Parry's affinity for the city in which she spent the first years of childhood: twenty extraordinary illustrations accompanied by her own hand-lettered prose — the story of "an odd bird" and his discovery of Paris.

MARIAN PARRY is an author, poet, illustrator and watercolour artist. Her books have been published by Knopf, Simon & Schuster, Greenwillow, Heritage Press and Limited Editions, Pharos Verlag (Switzerland) and Scholastic Books.

She has had numerous one-person shows. Her work is in the Metropolitan Museum of Art in New York, the Houghton Library of Harvard University and the Smith College Rare Book Room. The main archive of her work is in the print collection of the Boston Public Library.

Founder and senior instructor of the Watercolor Program for the Radcliffe Seminars at Harvard University, she was a fellow in the Bunting Fellowship Program, Radcliffe Institute.

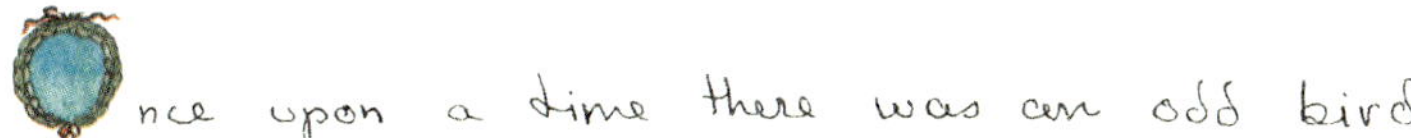

Once upon a time there was an odd bird

who could not endure the world as he found it.

Although he had lived all his life in America, he was convinced that everything was quite different in Europe, and that in Europe life was much more the way it ought to be.

He was sure that Europe was filled with a mysterious quality which made life, people, arts, cities, landscapes, houses, objects, foods, and everything else extraordinary, vivid, important, and beautiful.

"This is self-evident," he would say. "Look at the difference between

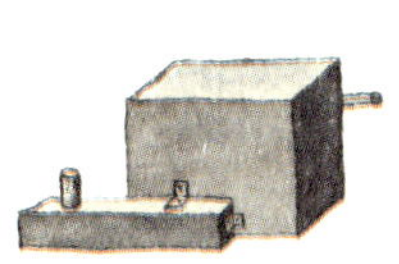
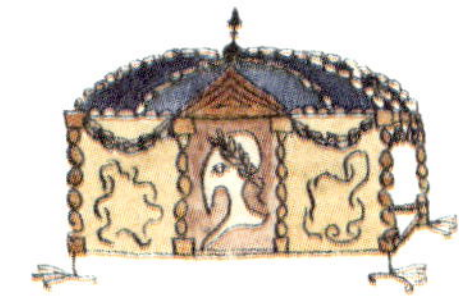
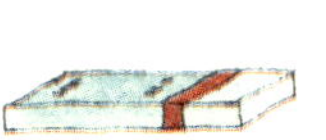
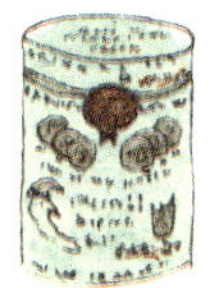

an American object and a European object, an American package and a European package,

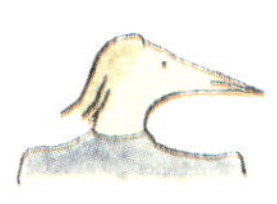
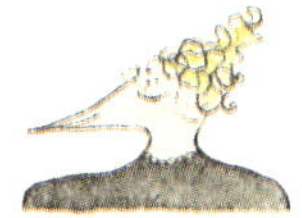
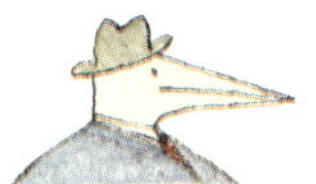
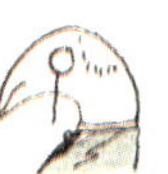

an American woman and a European woman, an American man and a European man,

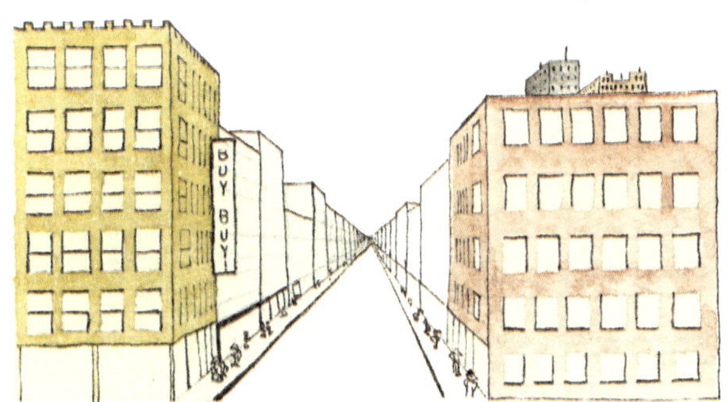

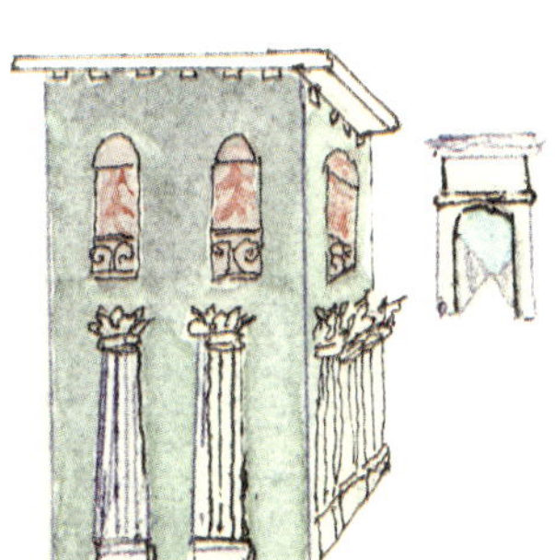
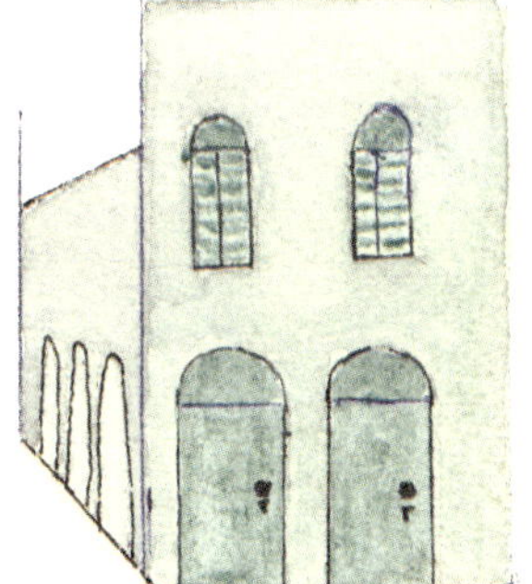

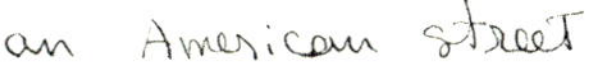
an American street and a European street..."

and so forth and so on.

"There are certain types of Americans," he would remark scornfully,

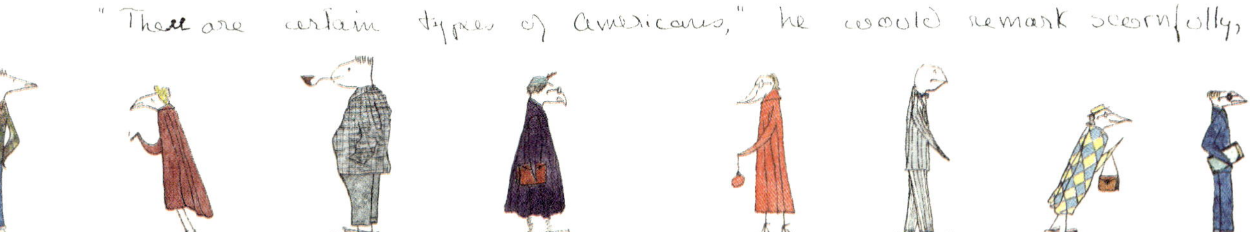

whom it would be incongruous and impossible to find in Europe."

Often he would talk with the vague, battered, people who had already been to Europe

and ask them questions.

But all they could ever say was, "Oh! It was wonderful, wonderful!" which made him realize that obviously their trips had been useless failures, and that in order to discover the transforming secret of Europe it was necessary for him to go there himself

When he had at last gathered together the requisite enormous sums of money, he set off for the place which itself was evidently a Europe in Europe. PARIS.

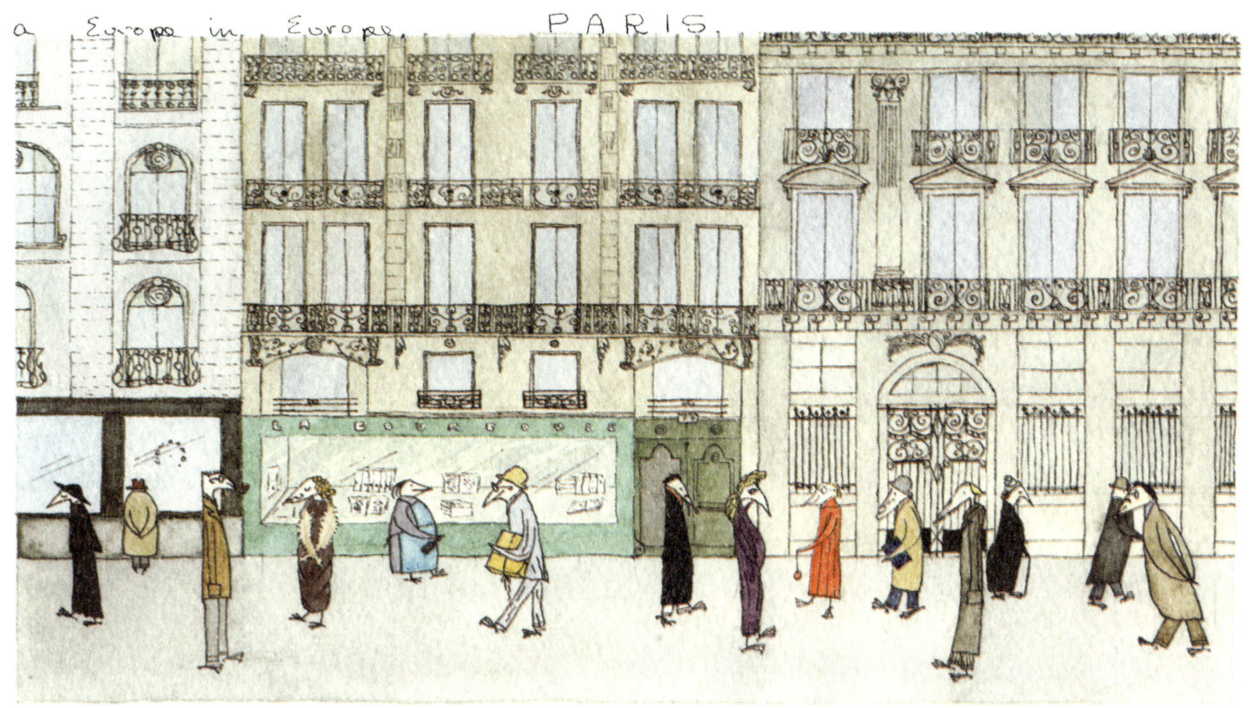

At first he did not know exactly what to do there.

He walked around the streets and looked at the people and the buildings.

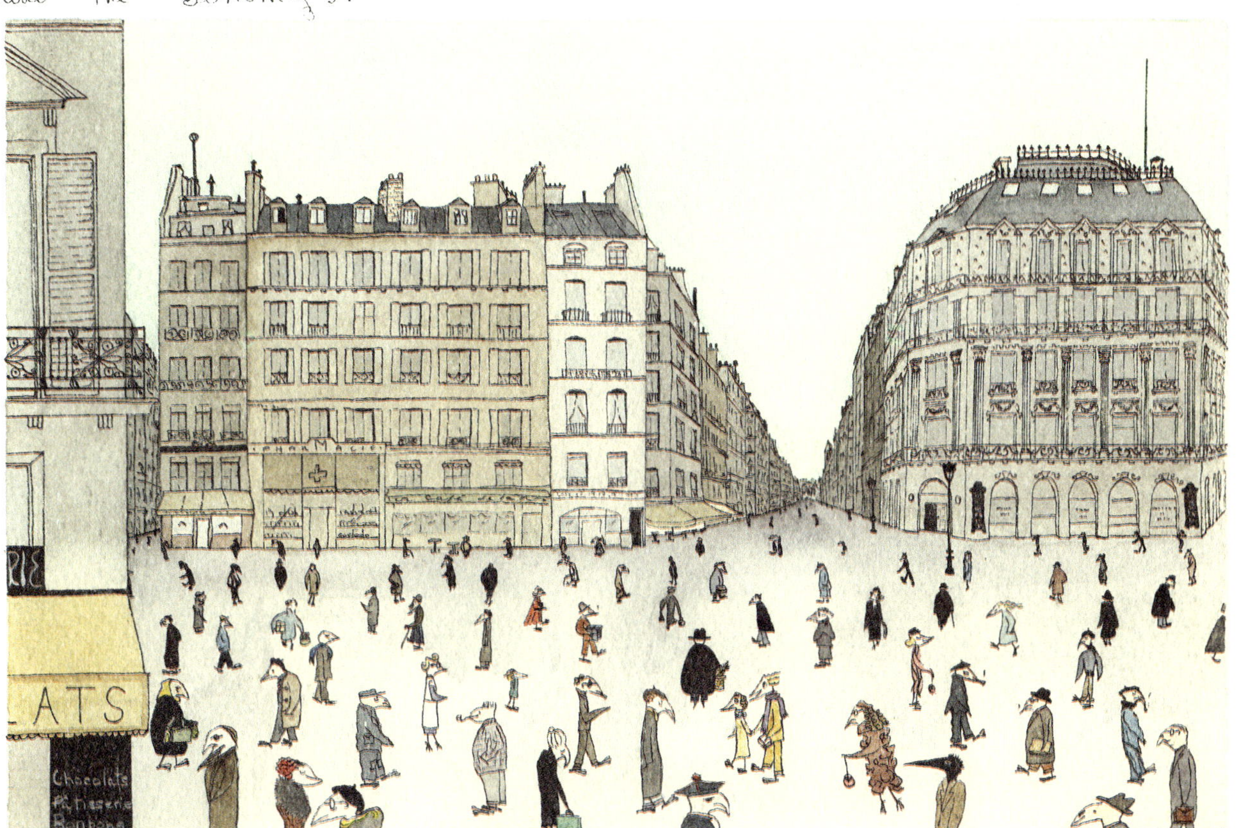

He walked in the parks.

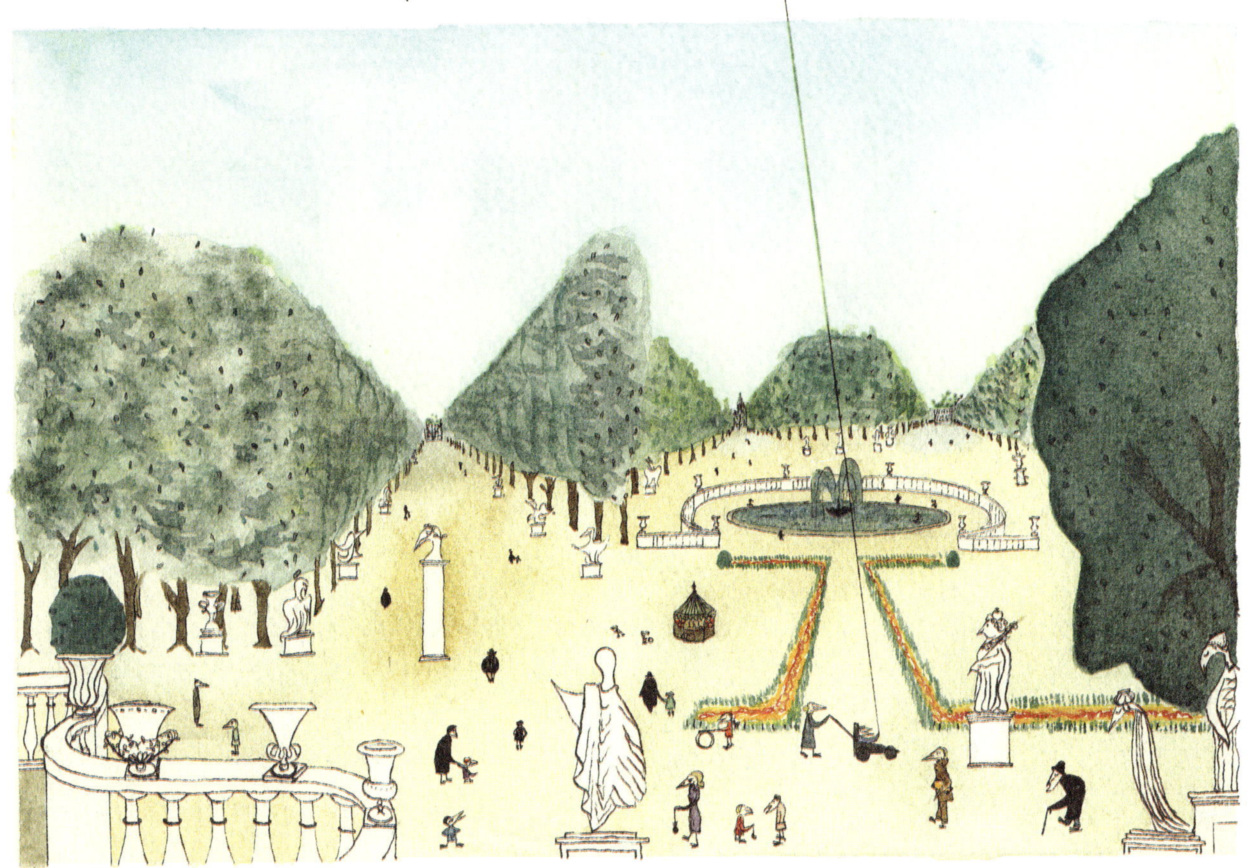

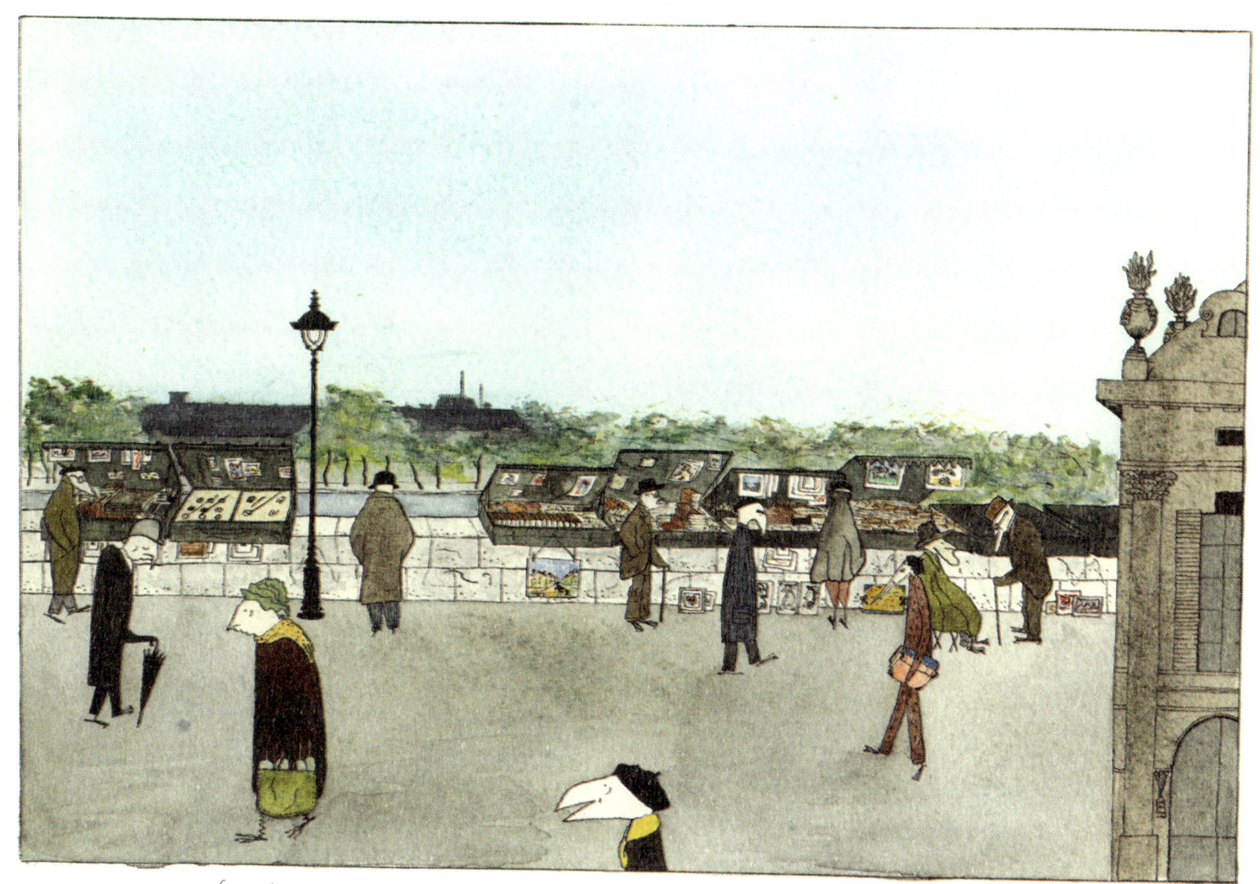

we walked by the Seine

Sometimes he would meet American aquaintances in a café.

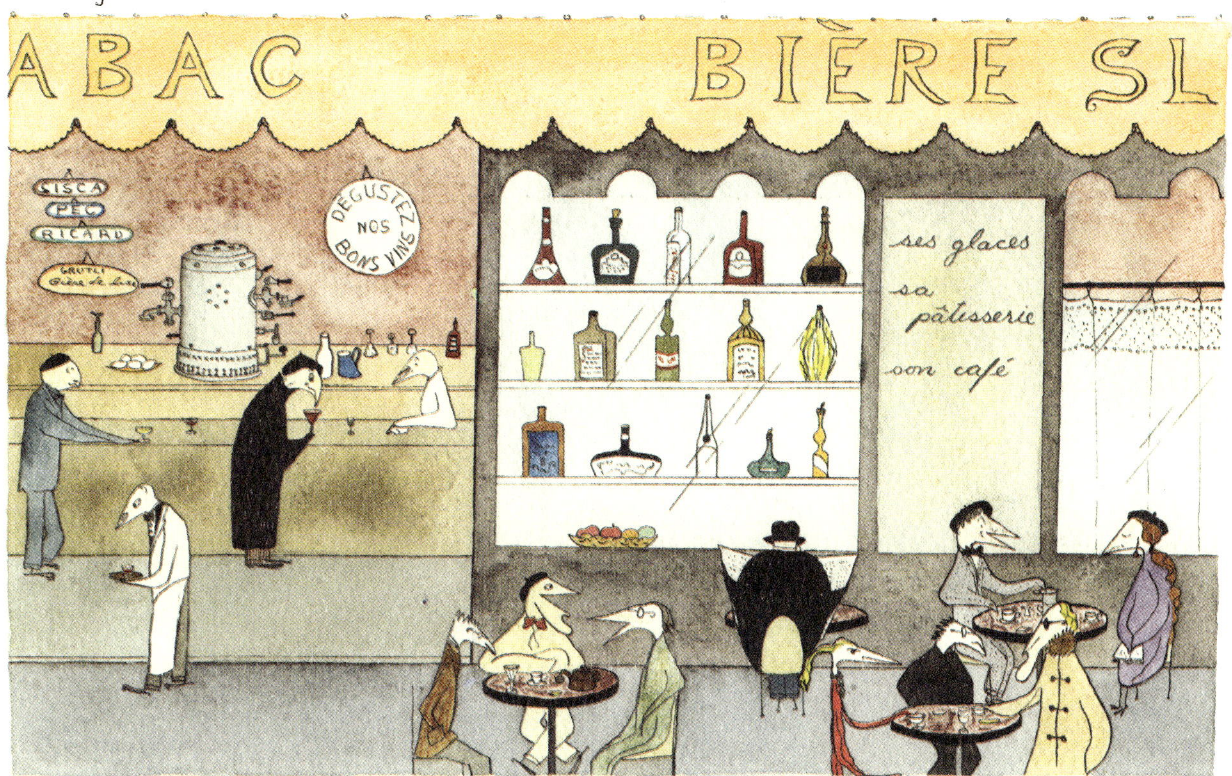

At last he began to learn how to live in Paris.

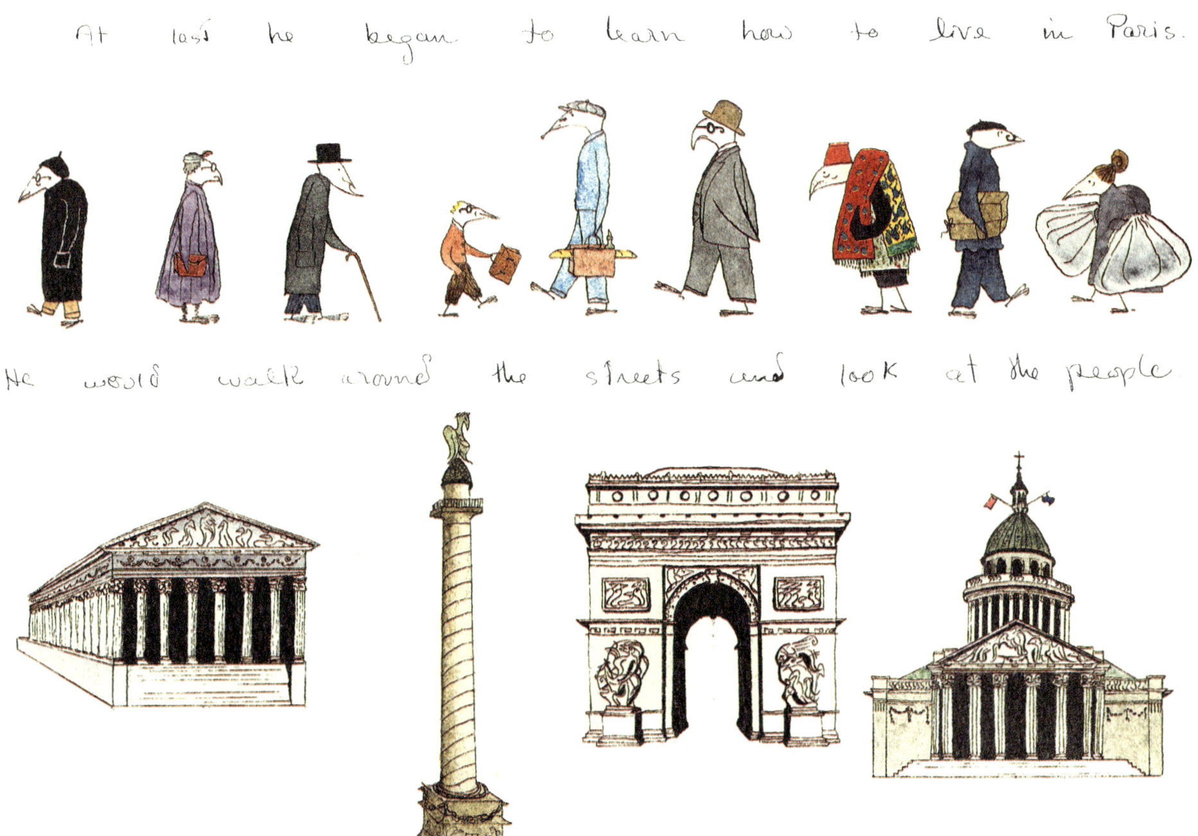

He would walk around the streets and look at the people

and the buildings.

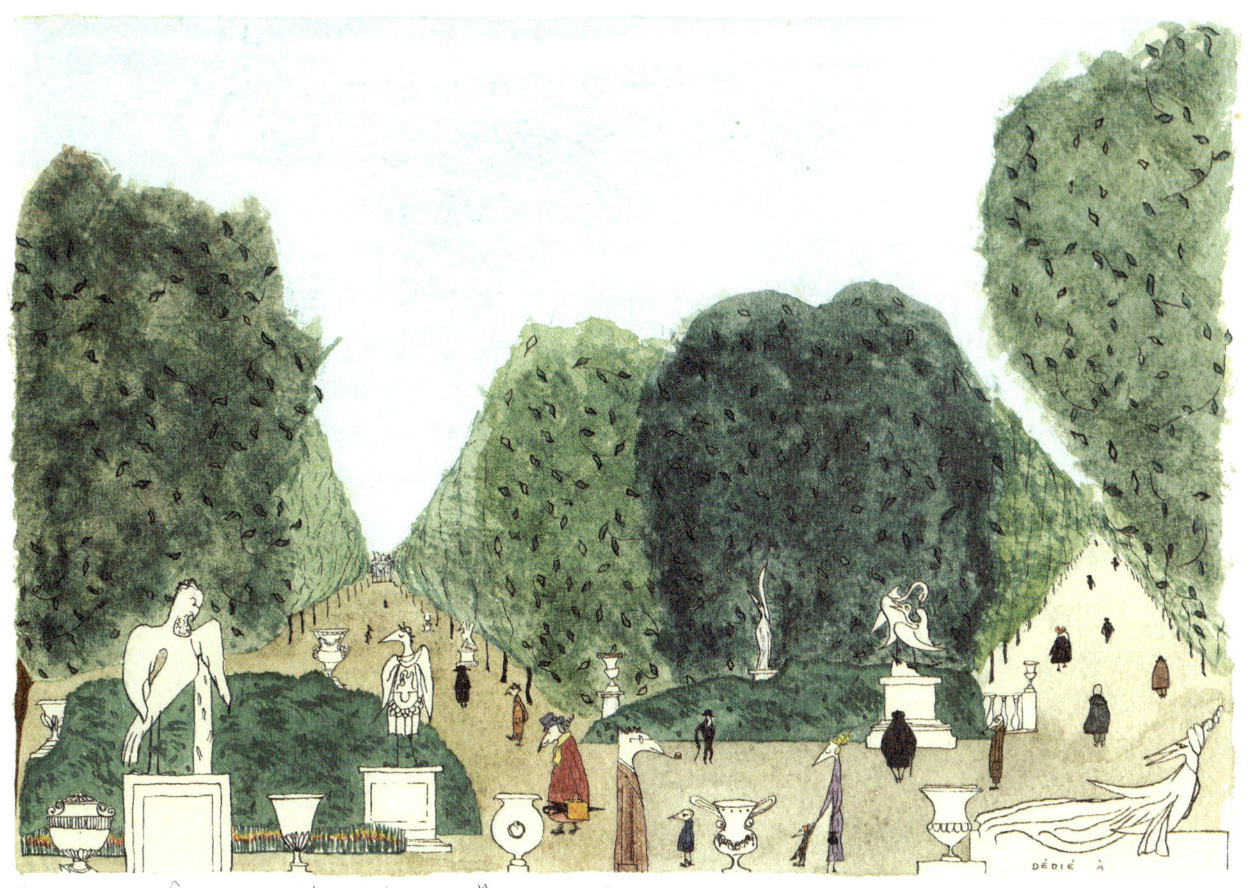

He would walk in the parks.

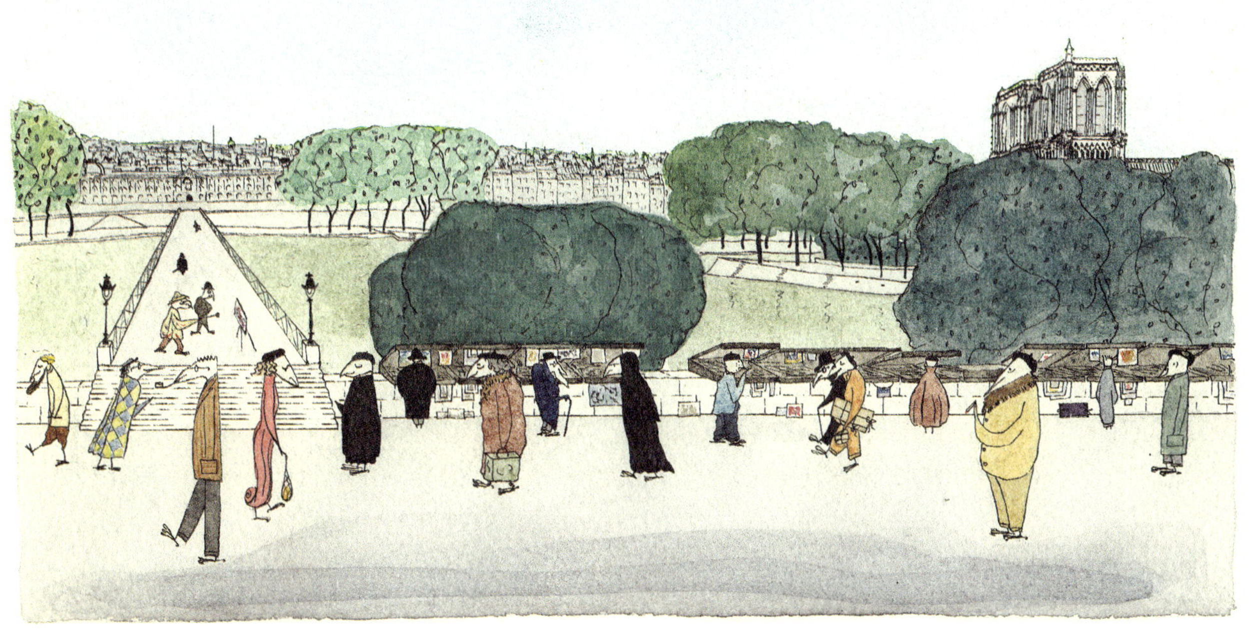

He would walk by the Seine.

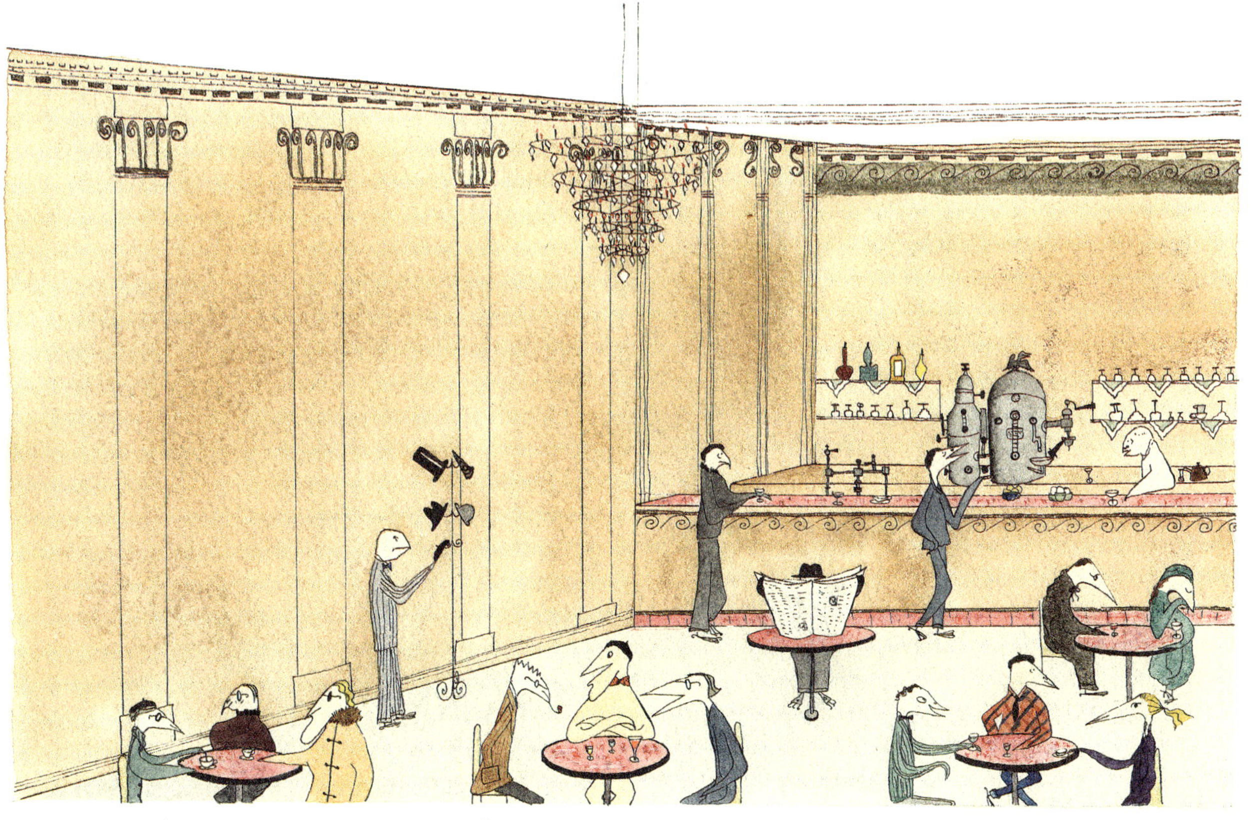

Sometimes he would meet French aquaintances in a café.

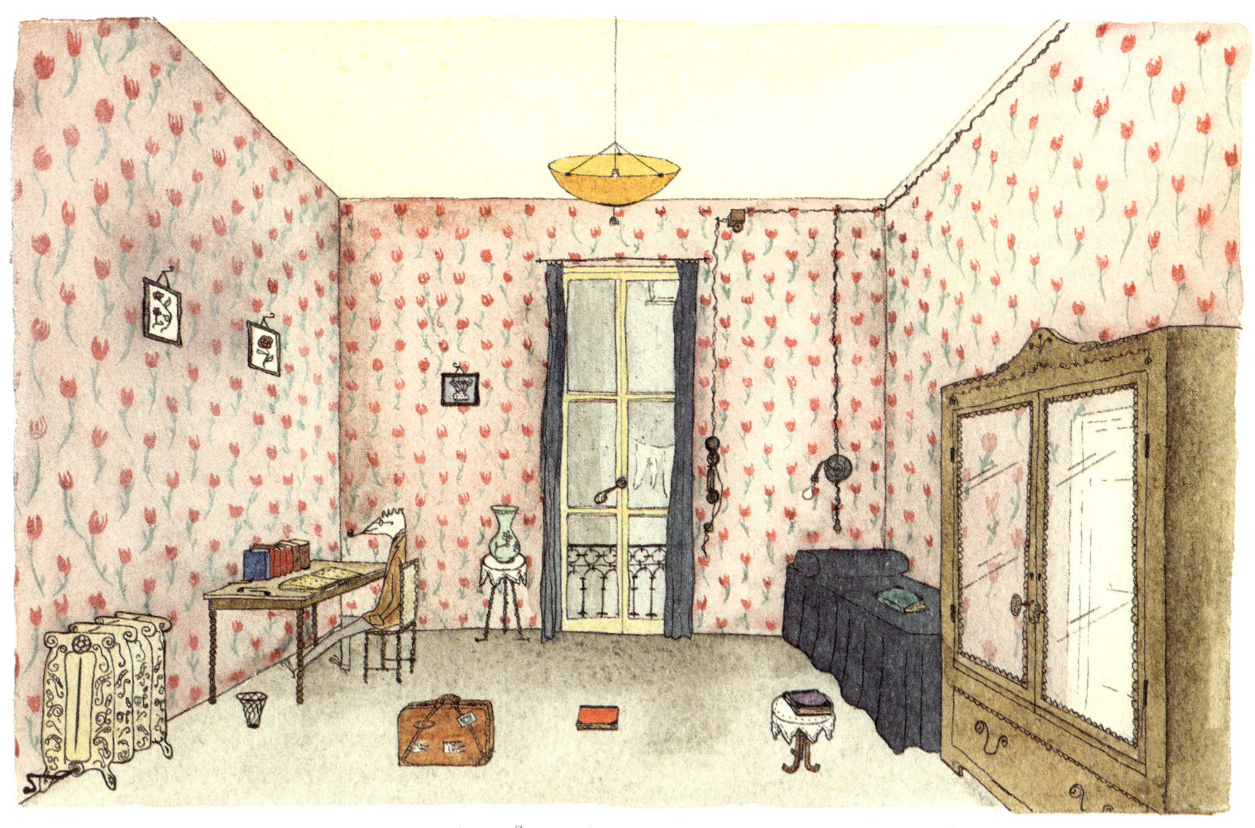

When he was tired he would stay in his hotel room.

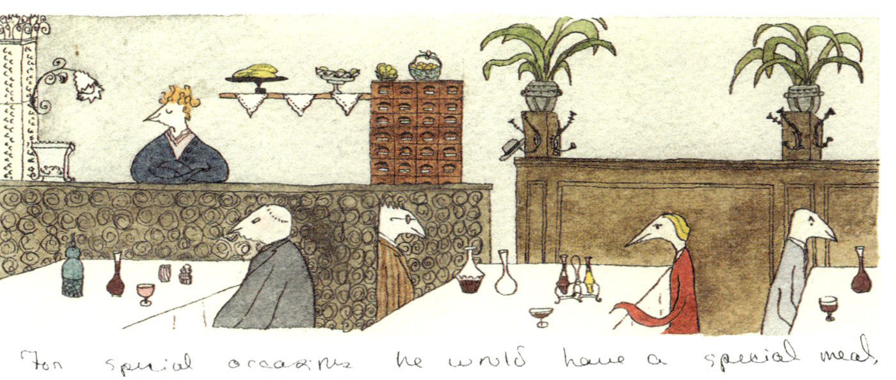

For special occasions he would have a special meal,

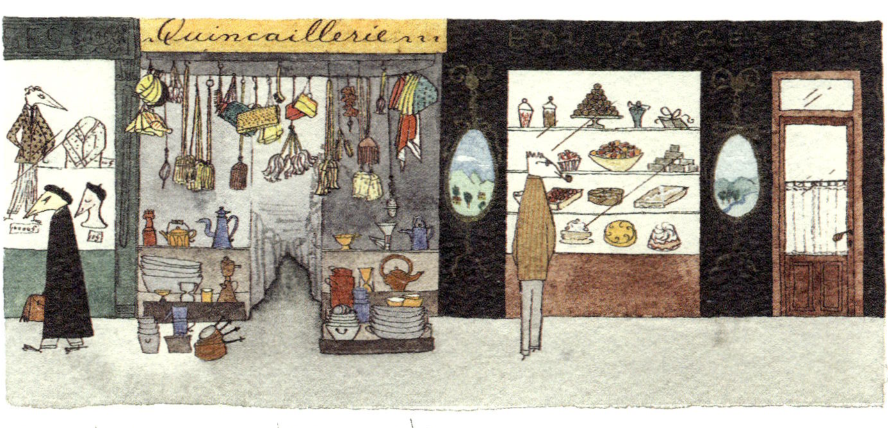

or look in shop windows,

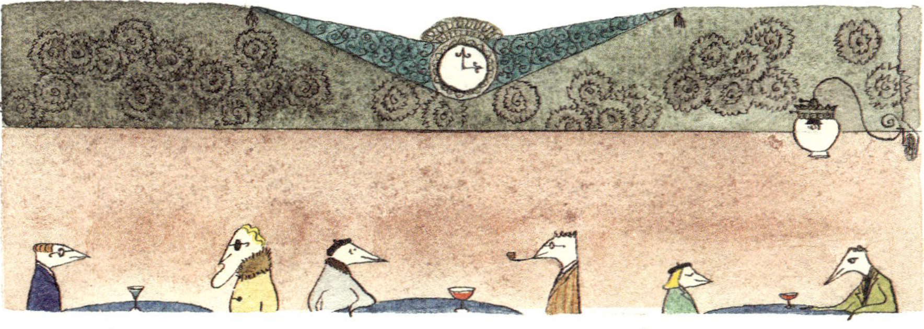

or drink aperitifs in a bistro and watch the people.

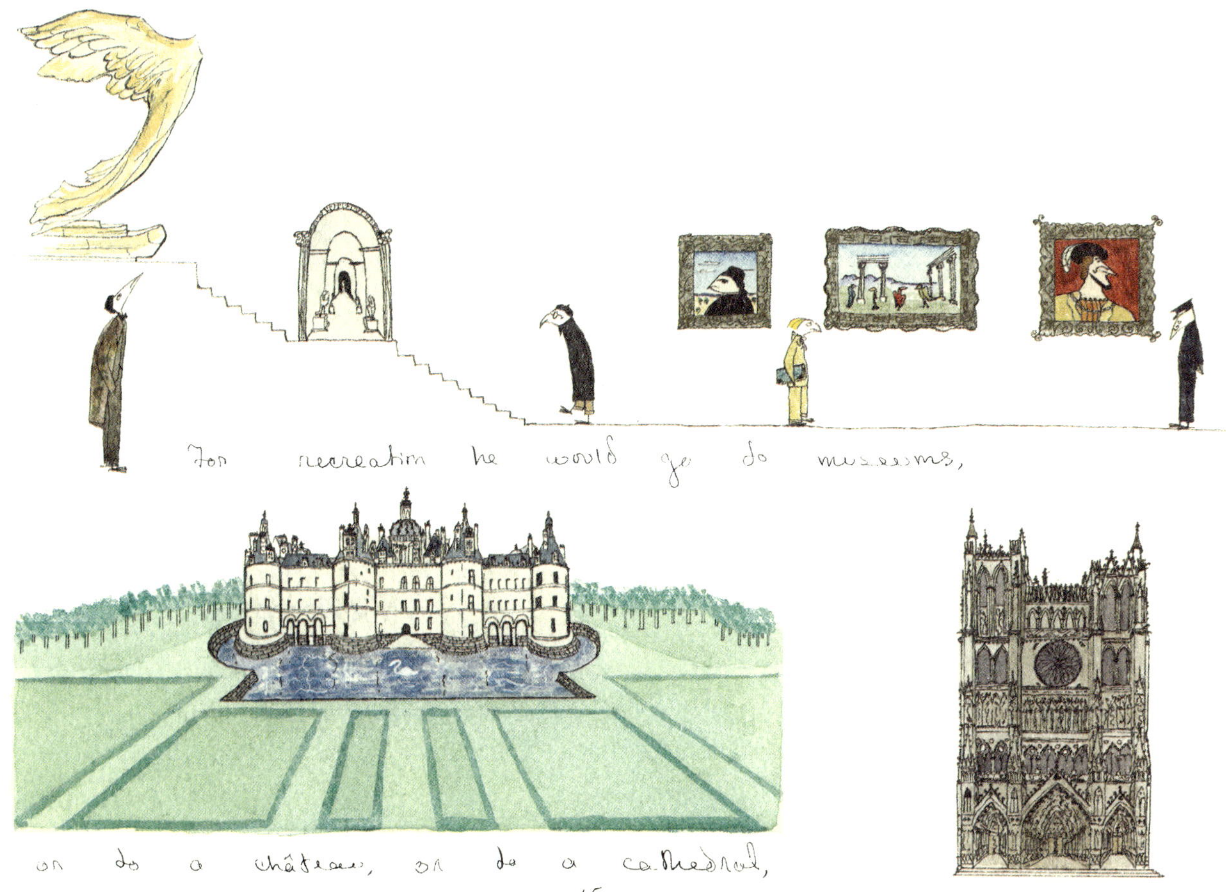

For recreation he would go to museums,

or to a château, or to a cathedral,

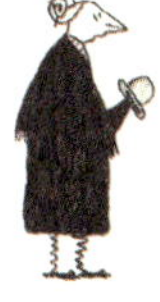

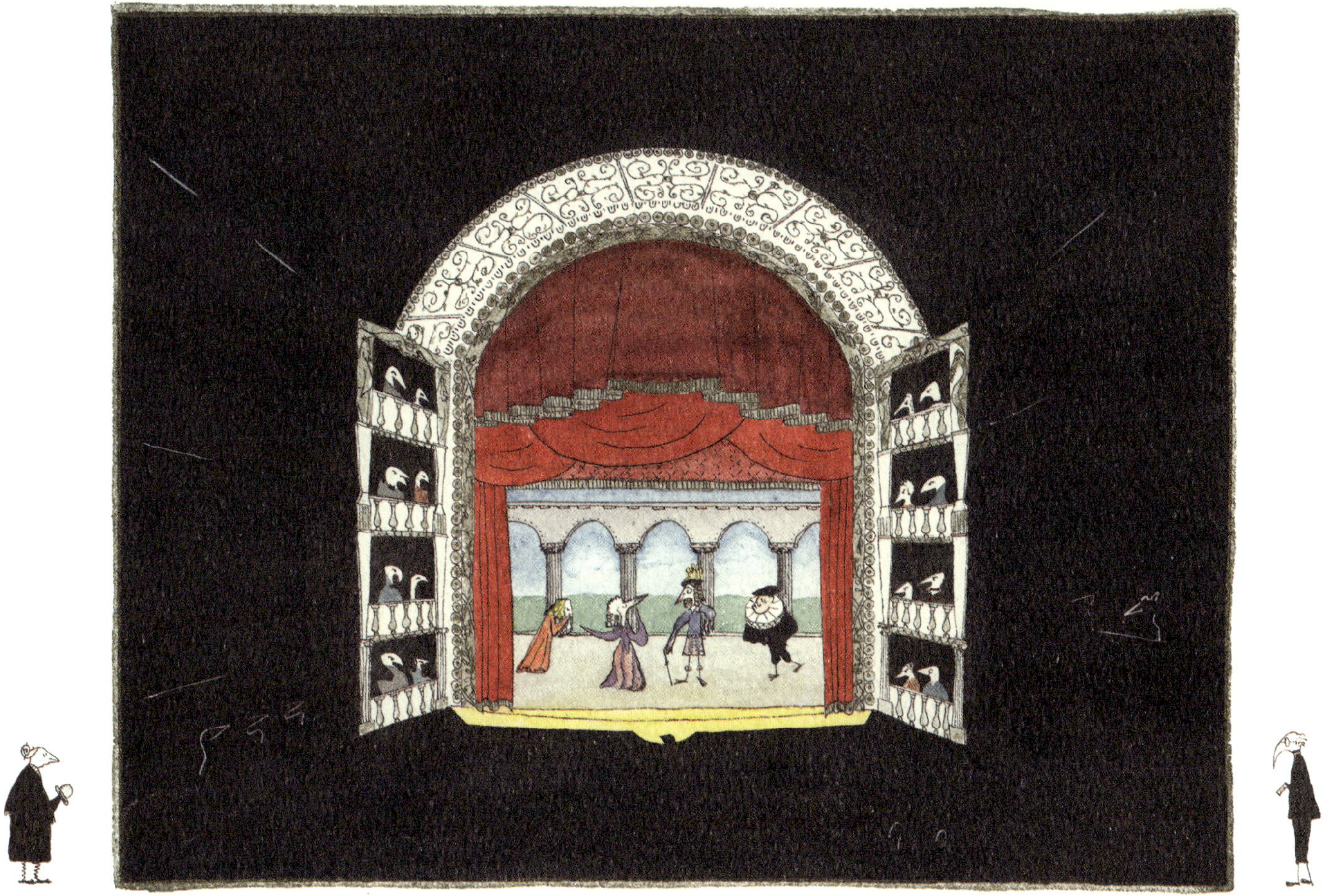

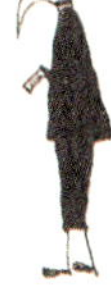

or to the theatre,

or walk in the streets and look at the people

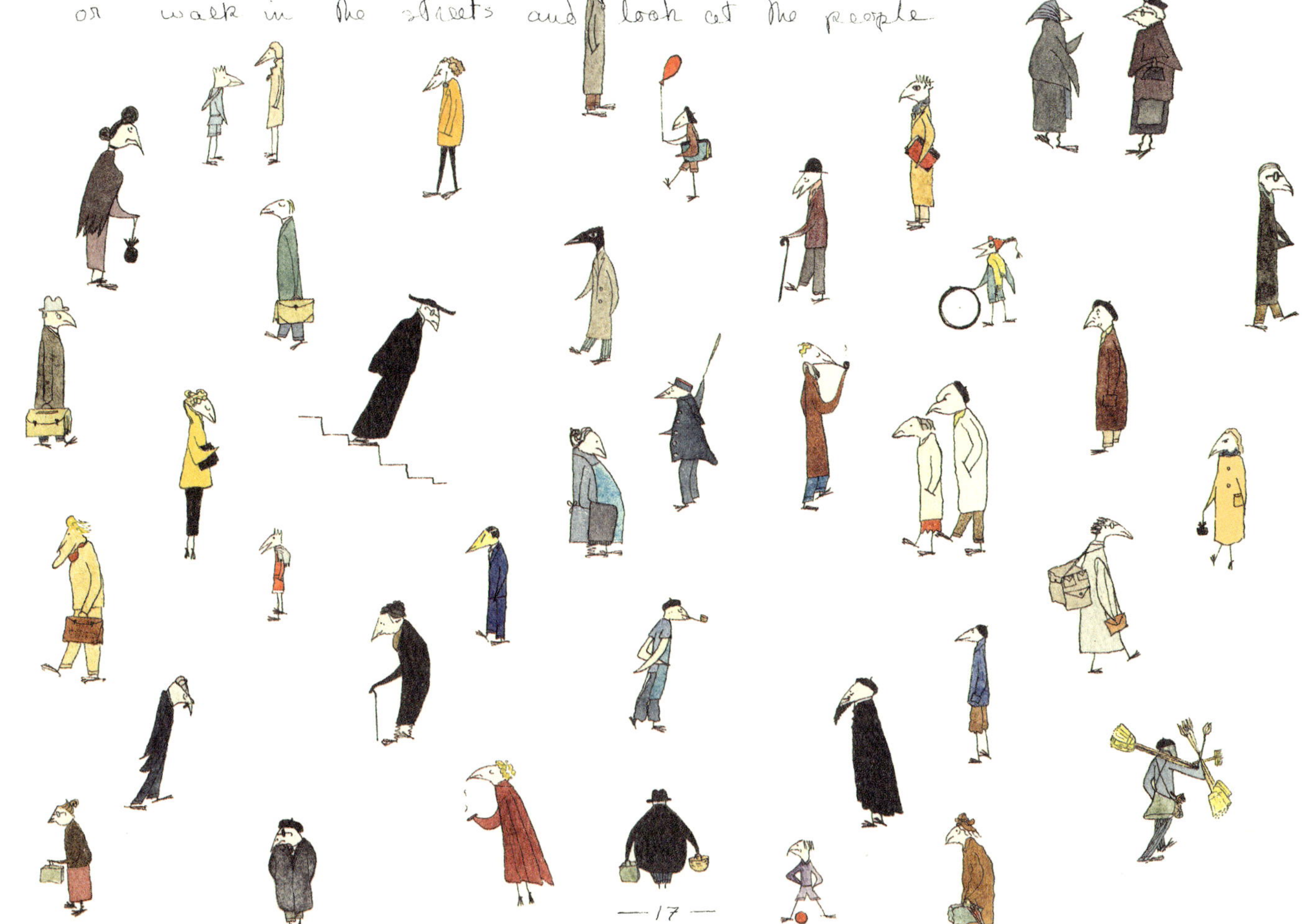

and the buildings,

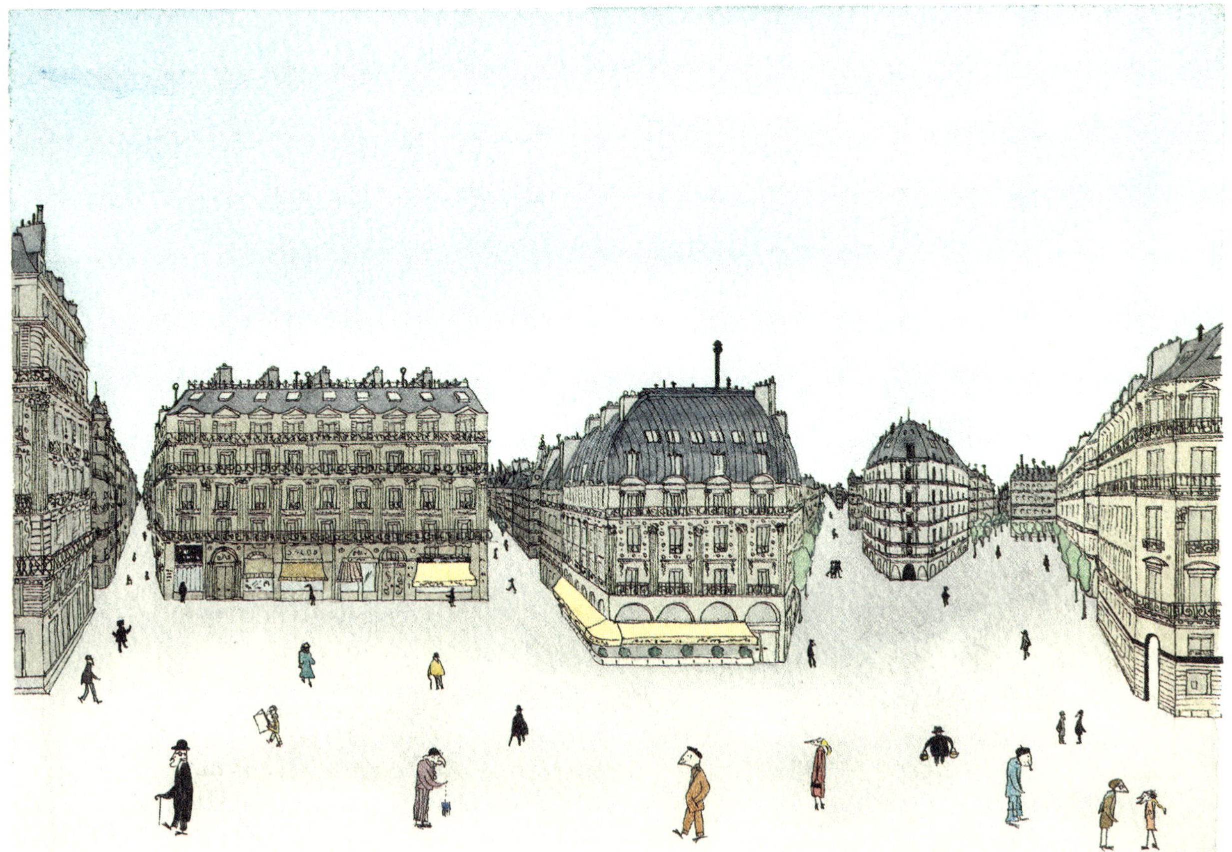

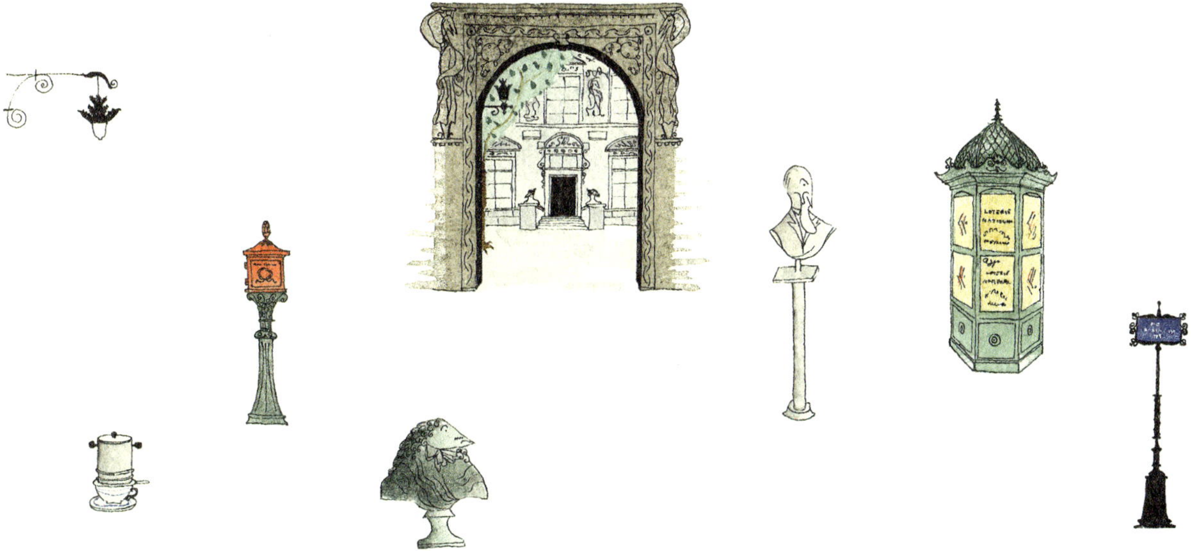

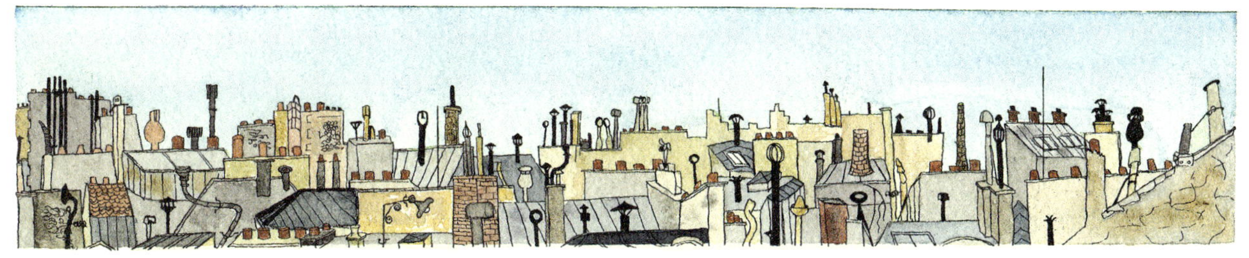

and this and that.

But no sooner had he learned to some extent how to live in Paris than he found all this money gone.

It was necessary for him to return to America.

When he arrived home, vague and battered,

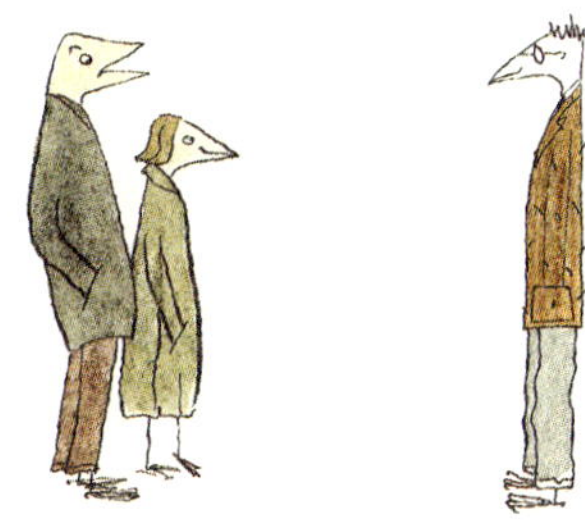

his friends questioned him about Europe. "Did you discover that "mysterious quality' you were always talking on about? Eh?" They kept asking him.

But he could find nothing to say except, "Ah! It was wonderful, wonderful!"

Fin

Un-Gyve Press is an independent imprint of The Un-Gyve Limited Group, publishing books of art, epicurism, literature, history, photography, industry, ephemera, etc. Christopher Ricks is the Literary Advisor to Un-Gyve.

The original illustrations in *The Paris Book* and the accompanying prose in the artist's hand were all-but completed in nineteen hundred and fifty two using Joseph Gillott 291 pen nibs and Higgins black India ink for the drawing and Winsor & Newton paints and brushes on the paper of a Canson & Montgolfier No. 0-7 grain fin watercolour block. Final touches were made by Marian Parry in late two thousand and twelve to bring this edition to print.

The text type used here is Garamond, D. Stempel AG, 1925, designed after the original types of Claude Garamond (c. 1480–1561). The paper is Strathmore Premium Grandee Felt.

Un-Gyve Press Boston
www.un-gyvepress.com

The Un-Gyve Limited Group
139A Charles Street, No. 393
Boston, Massachusetts 02114-3282 U.S.A.

The Paris Book, Marian Parry

Library of Congress Control Number: 2013958348
ISBN: 978-0-9829198-5-9

10 9 8 7 6 5 4 3 2 1